Elián González

Caught Between Two Countries

Frank Gresham

SCHOLASTIC INC.

New York   Toronto   London   Auckland   Sydney
Mexico City   New Delhi   Hong Kong   Buenos Aires

Developed by ONO Books in cooperation with Scholastic Inc.

ISBN 0-439-59796-X

8   9   10   23   12 11 10 09

Contents

Welcome to This Book

© Jeff Greenberg/Index Stock Imagery

Imagine floating on a rubber tube in the middle of the ocean. You are surrounded by sharks. And you are completely alone.

That's what happened to five-year-old Elián González in 1999. He was on a boat between Cuba and Florida. His mother was taking him to America. She wanted them to have a better life. But a storm hit the small boat.

Sound like a nightmare? It was just the beginning of Elián's amazing story.

Target Words

These words will help you understand what happened to Elián.

- **immigration:** moving to a new country to live

  Elián's case made people think about the laws that have to do with immigration.

- **opportunity:** the chance to do something

  Many people come to the United States to have greater opportunity.

- **protest:** a gathering of people who want to show how they feel about something

  Crowds in Florida held protests to try to keep Elián in the United States.

Reader Tips

Here's how to get the most from this book.

Photographs Photographs help you picture what is going on in a text. Look at the photograph of Elián on page 9. How does it help you understand what it was like for Elián to be rescued from the ocean?

Summarize A summary is a short statement about the most important ideas in a passage. As you read, summarize the most important points. It will help you better understand what you've read.

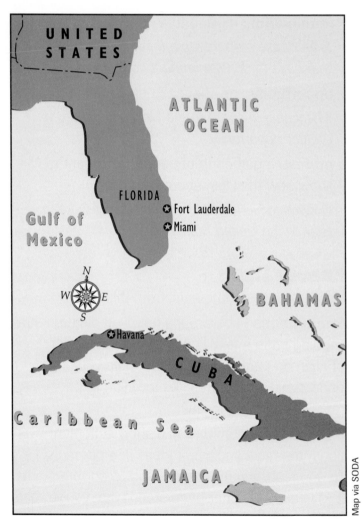

Cuba is only 90 miles south of Florida. But the waters are rough. And the trip can be a deadly one.

1

Rescued!

A boy is found floating in the ocean.

On Thanksgiving Day in 1999, two men were fishing from a small boat. They were fishing in the ocean near Fort Lauderdale, Florida. It was sunny and warm. The water was calm. Suddenly, they spotted something strange in the water. It looked like a doll had been tied to an **inner tube.** Dolphins were swimming around the inner tube, keeping sharks away. The fishermen moved closer to get a better look.

They were shocked to see it was no doll. It was a small boy. And he was barely alive. He was shivering and moaning. He begged for something to drink. The men quickly pulled him into their boat. They gave him some water and rushed him to shore.

A Mystery

At the hospital, doctors looked at the boy. His skin was cut and scratched. He was also **dehydrated.** He needed water badly. But the doctors said he would be fine.

The boy spoke only Spanish. He said that he had been on a boat with his mom. He said a wave knocked them off the boat. And he said his name was Elián. Elián González. The question was—who did he belong to?

Heads Up!

How did Elián get rescued? Retell what happened in your own words.

This picture of Elián was taken a few days after his rescue.

Escape From Cuba

A mystery is solved.

Soon after Elián was found, a man and a woman washed up alive onto the beach near Miami. They had been in the water for the same amount of time as Elián. They spoke Spanish, like Elián. They said they were survivors of a **shipwreck**. So U.S. government officials went to the hospital to talk to them. They were hoping to find out what had happened to the boy.

Here's what the officials learned. Three days before Thanksgiving, 14 people had left the island of **Cuba** in a small boat. They were headed for Florida, which was ninety miles away.

This was a dangerous trip for such a small boat. The boat was only 16 feet long. The waters between Cuba and Florida can get very rough.

The boat left Cuba very early in the morning. With luck, it would reach Florida that night. But soon after it set sail, the boat's motor died. The group returned to Cuba to fix it. The repairs did not take long. The boat set sail again.

A Storm Comes

The boat moved very slowly. It was carrying a heavy load of people. And the motor was small.

Late in the morning, dark clouds filled the sky. It looked like a storm was about to start. And the little boat was headed right for it.

The boat's passengers were in trouble, and they knew it. The winds picked up. The waves got higher. Some passengers prayed. Some just hoped for the best. It was all they could do.

The storm hit them hard. Strong winds came first. Pelting rain came next. The boat bobbed in the water like a beach ball.

Heads Up!

How did the passengers know they were in trouble?

The passengers thought they might be able to wait out the storm. They were not far from Florida. If only they could make it a few miles farther north!

High waves splashed water into the boat. The passengers got wet. Then the waves got higher and rushed over the boat's sides. The passengers tried to scoop out the water. But it was coming in too fast. They could not keep the water out.

Then things got worse. The boat's motor died. Now they weren't even moving forward.

The boat began to drift. It went wherever the waves pushed it. Wave after wave sent water crashing into the boat.

It was not long before the boat was full of water. It was going to sink, and everybody on board knew it.

Heads Up!

What did the government officials learn about Elián?

Quick Facts About Cuba

Cuba is

- about the size of Pennsylvania.
- an island in the Caribbean Sea.
- a **communist** country ruled by Fidel Castro.
  He has been in charge since 1959. Castro also
  heads Cuba's only legal political party, the
  Communist Party.

Cuba has

- a capital city named Havana.
- more than 11,225,000 citizens.
- money called pesos (PAY-sos).
- a bad relationship with the United States.
  The U.S. is against communism.

Cubans

- can expect to live about 77 years, just
  as long as North Americans.
- earn, on average, about $240 a month.
- celebrate Independence Day on December 10.
  It was on that day in 1898 that Cuba won its
  freedom from Spain.

3

Under the Waves

Death comes first, then a miracle.

There were no **life preservers** on the boat. But the group had brought two large inner tubes with them. They were for Elián and some of the adults who couldn't swim.

Water flooded into the small boat. Soon, everyone was up to their necks in water. Some of them grabbed hold of the inner tubes as they floated by. Others started swimming. In minutes, the boat had dropped beneath the waves.

Those who were holding onto the inner tubes were unable to reach the others. The waves were too rough. All they could do was watch their friends sink below the surface of the water and drown. The strong waves soon carried the inner tubes away.

A man and a woman were able to keep hold of one of the inner tubes. Elián's mother was holding onto the other one. She tied Elián to the top of it. Then a wave knocked her away. She did not come back.

To Safety

After a while, the clouds lifted. The waves died down. Elián was on his own. He had lived through the storm. But he had no food or water. Surely he would die in the shark-filled waters.

For two days, Elián drifted. And then a miracle happened. The men who were out fishing spotted the inner tube. Minutes later, they pulled Elián to safety.

—Heads Up!—

What happened after the boat sank and before Elián was rescued?

A Common Struggle

Why would 14 people risk their lives in a small boat to leave Cuba and come to America?

The truth is that thousands of people do so every year. One of the most famous is the pitcher Orlando Hernandez, "El Duque." He came because he wanted to play baseball. Hernandez had been banned from playing in Cuba after his brother ran away to the U.S.

Most people come to the U.S. for freedom and opportunity. That's because the United States is a **democracy.** People elect their leaders. And if they don't like what their leaders do, they are free to criticize them.

People can also get their news from any newspaper or TV station they like. And they can travel freely.

Cubans don't have all these freedoms. Cubans can elect their lawmakers. But their choices are limited. All of the **candidates** must be members of the Communist Party. Cubans can also vote for president. But there is only one candidate— Fidel Castro. So Cubans who don't like him aren't free to vote for someone else.

People who live in Cuba are not allowed to criticize the government. Their news is controlled by the government. And people are not allowed to leave the country unless the government says they can. If the government thinks that a person will not return to Cuba, the person is not allowed to leave.

Cubans who want to leave sometimes escape on small boats. It's dangerous. But to them, it is worth the risk.

Elián's mother wanted to leave. She had always dreamed of living in America. Elián's father did not want to leave. But they were divorced. And Elián's mother did not tell his father that she wanted to take Elián.

Elián's mother broke the law. But she thought what she was doing was right. She wanted her son to grow up in a free country.

The year Elián González came to America, over 1,300 other Cubans set out for Florida in small boats. At least 60 of them died.

4

Tug-of-War

Who gets Elián?

The news spread fast throughout Miami. Before long, everyone was talking about Elián and the shipwreck.

Elián had relatives in Miami. They had heard the news as well. Elián's great-uncle Lázaro González rushed to the hospital. He was thrilled that Elián was alive.

That night, the relatives phoned Elián's father in Cuba. He had been very worried. For four days he had no news of Elián. Now he knew his son was safe. He was overjoyed. He asked when Elián would be coming home.

That was a question the relatives did not want to answer. They were not sure what to do with Elián. Should they try to keep him in Miami? Or should they send him back to his father in Cuba?

Fidel Castro (left) and Elián's father, Juan Miguel González, wanted Elián to return to Cuba.

A Difficult Problem

For Elián's dad, Juan Miguel, the answer was simple. Elián belonged in Cuba with him. But Lázaro and his family wanted Elián to stay in Miami. It was, after all, what his mother had wanted. The two men argued over the phone. But they could not agree.

Lázaro's family had left Cuba when Castro took over. Lázaro loved the freedoms in America. He wanted Elián to have those freedoms, too.

Elián's Uncle Lázaro (left) wanted to keep Elián in the United States.

© AFP/Corbis

Lázaro believed that the law was on his side. Special laws protect Cubans who escape to the United States. Lázaro believed that those laws would let him keep Elián.

Elián's father did not care about any special laws. The law had nothing to do with it, he said. Elián had watched his mother die. He needed to be with his father.

Elián's father did not think that Elián would have a better life in the United States. Elián had lived a happy life in Cuba, his father said. Cuba was his home. If Elián returned, he would be happy again.

By then, Elián was living in Lázaro's house. He didn't know about the argument. But people all over the United States and Cuba did. Soon people everywhere were taking sides.

What would happen next?

Heads Up!

What would your decision be? Would you let Elián stay in the U.S. as his mother had wanted? Or would you send him back to Cuba to be with his father?

5

Clash in Miami

The United States government steps in.

Some people found it easy to decide whether Elián should return to Cuba or stay in Miami. Most of these people had strong feelings about Castro or the United States. But for many others, the decision was not so easy.

Elián himself wasn't old enough to decide. He had just turned six. And a six-year-old child cannot make **legal** decisions. In the United States, parents make those decisions. In some cases, another family member might be able to make legal decisions, too. But only if the child had no parents. Elián still had a father.

Elián's family in Miami were distant relatives. But they were hoping they would be able to make a strong enough case to keep Elián here.

A Safe Home

The United States grants **asylum**, or protection, to people who are in danger from their own governments. People who apply for asylum can become **legal residents** in the United States. They may become United States citizens later, if they want.

But a special law says that Cubans can become legal residents just by staying in the United States for a year. The U.S. Congress passed that law in 1966. Lázaro wanted the government to grant Elián asylum right away. Otherwise, Lázaro would try to keep Elián in Miami for a year.

The United States **Immigration** and **Naturalization** Service, or INS, decides who can stay in the country legally and who can't. So it was up to the INS to try and settle the argument between Elián's father and his great-uncle.

What would they decide?

—Heads Up!—

What do you think the INS will say about Elián's case?

6

The Long Wait

The world watches Elián.

INS officials took their time. They did not want to make any mistakes. They studied the laws. They spoke with Lázaro. They flew to Cuba to talk with Elián's father.

Fidel Castro wanted Elián back right away. Thousands marched in Cuba. They held up posters with Elián's picture. They screamed and chanted. Their posters read "Bring Elián Back!"

In Miami, Cuban Americans staged **protests,** too. Like people in Cuba, they wanted the INS to decide fast. They wanted the INS to say that Elián could stay in the United States. They passed out **flyers** that asked for support. They wore T-shirts with Elián's face on them. They helped get Elián's story heard around the world.

The Decision

While everyone waited, Lázaro and his family took care of Elián. They took him to parks. They bought him toys. Someone gave him a puppy. Elián's family in Florida tried to give him a normal American life.

It was not easy. Groups of people gathered outside their home in Miami every day. TV camera crews lined up. It had been a month, and Elián's story was still big news.

On January 5, INS officials finally announced their decision. They said the boy should go home. The INS agreed that Elián might have a better future in the United States. But they decided that he needed his father's care.

"This little boy, who has been through so much," an official said, "belongs with his father."

Lázaro's family was heartbroken. People in Miami could not believe it. They were **furious**. Thousands of protesters marched in the streets. They carried signs that said "Freedom!" and "Let Him Stay!"

Angry protesters in Miami expressed their feelings about the decision to send Elián back to Cuba.

There were protests in Cuba, too. The biggest one was in Elián's hometown. Thousands of people gathered there. They had a message for the American government. They said they wanted Elián to come home now.

It was a complicated situation. The U.S. government was feeling the pressure.

Heads Up!

Why did the INS say that Elián should go home? Do you agree or disagree? Why?

The Waiting Ends

Would the U.S. government change its decision?

The INS had decided that Elián should go back to Cuba. But that's not what happened. Instead, Lázaro took the case to court. He asked the court to make the INS change its mind.

At that time, Janet Reno was the United States attorney general. She ran the United States Department of Justice. It was her job to **enforce** America's laws.

In late January, Elián's two grandmothers came to the United States from Cuba. They went to Washington, D.C. They met with Janet Reno and other government leaders. They flew to Miami and spent a few hours with Elián. But they went back to Cuba without him.

Reno agreed with the INS. She said Elián should go back to Cuba. But she said she would let the courts decide. So the waiting continued.

Worrying About Elián

How did Elián feel? In late March, a TV reporter spoke with Elián. Elián talked about how the boat sank. He said he did not believe his mother was dead.

"She must have been picked up here in Miami somewhere," he said. "She must have lost her memory, and just doesn't know I'm here."

He did not want to return to Cuba, he said. But he did not like Miami, either. Clearly, Elián was a confused little boy. Some experts watched him talk. They thought he needed help to deal with his loss. They were worried about him.

Juan Miguel was worried about his son, too. But Elián could not leave the United States. He had to stay until the court made a decision.

Finally, Elián's dad flew to the United States to be with his son. He brought his wife and their baby boy, Elián's half brother.

Castro let Juan Miguel and his family go to the U.S. because they promised they would all return to Cuba after the court case was settled. Meanwhile, Elián would stay with them.

But Lázaro and his family didn't want to let go of Elián. They did not trust Juan Miguel. They were afraid he would take Elián back to Cuba right away.

Janet Reno went to Miami on April 12. She met with Elián's relatives. She told them they had to give the boy up. But Lázaro's family still refused.

Elián's father was running out of **patience.** By April 20, he had been in the United States for two weeks. But he had not yet seen Elián.

Juan Miguel spoke to the press. He asked all Americans to help him get his son back. Still, Lázaro's family would not give Elián to his father.

Heads Up!

Look up the word patience *in the glossary. Why do you think Elián's father was running out of patience?*

Federal agents take Elián from his Miami relatives' home.

Breaking Down the Door

It was early in the morning on April 22. Lázaro had been up all night talking with government officials. He had finally fallen asleep. Other people in the house were awake. Elián was one of them. He could not sleep.

Suddenly the front door crashed open. The family looked up. Men wearing helmets and goggles stormed in. They carried guns. They worked for the INS, and they had come to take Elián.

A family friend grabbed Elián. He carried the boy into a bedroom and locked the door. The men with the helmets and guns broke it down.

The friend carried Elián into a closet. But there was nowhere to hide. The special agents grabbed the boy. They carried him outside to a waiting van. In a moment, they were gone.

Heads Up!

How do you think Elián felt when the INS officers took him away?

Where Do You Stand?

Should Elián be sent back to Cuba?

Read these two arguments. Then decide which side has the best case.

No! Elián should stay in Miami!

Elián's mother wanted him to have a better life. The U.S. should make sure he gets it. In Cuba, few jobs pay well. In America, there is more **opportunity.** In Cuba, it is not safe to speak out against the government. In America, it is. Let's face it, the United States is the land of freedom. Cuba is not. Sending Elián back there would be unfair to him.

Yes! Elián should go back to Cuba!

Sure, America offers many things that Cuba doesn't offer. But one thing it doesn't have is Elián's family. This young boy's mother just died. He needs his father and his grandparents.

Also, Elián's mother took him on a dangerous trip without telling Elián's father. She had no right to do that. Elián was happy in Cuba. If he were allowed to go home, he'd be happy again.

8

Elián's Return

Elián goes from Miami to Maryland to Cuba.

INS agents flew with Elián to an airport near Washington, D.C. When Elián got off the plane, he was surprised. His father was waiting for him. He hugged his father and did not let go.

Back in Miami, Cuban Americans woke up and turned on their TV sets. News of the raid made them angry. They went out into the streets and yelled. Some people were so mad they stopped traffic. Some burned tires. Some got arrested. They all wanted Elián back.

Out of the Spotlight

Elián and his family moved into a farmhouse in Maryland. Reporters and TV cameras were kept away. For the first time in five months, Elián was out of the news.

The change seemed to do him good. Photos taken at the time show him relaxed and happy. Four classmates from his school in Cuba came for a visit. His kindergarten teacher came, too.

It took the courts two months to decide Elián's case. In the end, the INS won. Elián could go home. On June 28, he and his dad got on a plane.

"We are very happy to go home," his father said. "Thank you."

Elián González is back in Cuba with his father, stepmother, and half brother.

© AP Photo/Courtesy of Juan Miguel Gonzalez

A few hours later, they landed in Havana, Cuba's capital. About eight hundred children from Elián's school were there to greet him. They waved red, white, and blue Cuban flags. "Elián! Elián! Elián!" they yelled. When his father carried him off the plane, they cheered. Elián had been away for seven months.

Back in Miami, people still talk about Elián. They miss him. Lázaro's house is a museum now. Visitors can see Elián's clothes and toys. And they can see the inner tube that saved his life.

The Cubans have set up a museum for Elián, too. It is in Cardenas, the town where Elián lives with his father, stepmother, and younger brothers. The museum's main attraction is a statue of a little boy. The boy is Elián González.

—Heads Up!—

What do you think life is like now in Cuba for Elián?

Glossary

asylum *(noun)* protection given by a country to people escaping danger in their own country and who might be harmed if they return (p. 23)

candidate *(noun)* someone who is running for office (p. 16)

communist *(adjective)* having the belief that a nation's people should own all land and businesses together and that all profits should be shared (p. 13)

Cuba *(noun)* an island and a nation ninety miles south of Florida (p. 10)

dehydrated *(adjective)* dried out (p. 8)

democracy *(noun)* a system of government in which leaders are freely elected (p. 16)

enforce *(verb)* to make sure that a law is obeyed (p. 28)

flyer *(noun)* a paper with a message written on it (p. 24)

furious *(adjective)* extremely angry (p. 25)

immigration *(noun)* moving to a new country to live (p. 23)

Glossary

inner tube *(noun)* a rubber ring filled with air. It goes inside a tire. (p. 7)

legal *(adjective)* having to do with laws (p. 22)

legal resident *(noun)* someone who has permission to live and work in the United States (p. 23)

life preserver *(noun)* a belt, vest, or ring that can be filled with air and used to keep people afloat in water (p. 14)

naturalization *(noun)* the act of making someone a citizen of a country (p. 23)

opportunity *(noun)* the chance to do something (p. 33)

patience *(noun)* the quality of putting up with problems and delays without getting angry (p. 30)

protest *(noun)* a gathering of people who want to show how they feel about something (p. 24)

shipwreck *(noun)* the sinking of a boat or ship (p. 10)

Index